THE ULTIMATE

FLYING MACHINES

SOCIAL MEDIA MODELERS REFERENCE MANUAL

Written & Compiled by
Donald Semora

Published Through
CASTLE TOP GROUP

THE ULTIMATE FLYING MACHINES
SOCIAL MEDIA MODELERS REFERENCE MANUAL

Copyright 2020

Written by Donald Semora
Book Cover by Donald Semora
Book Layout and Design by Donald Semora

ISBN NUMBER
978-1-940155-88-3

Book is designed and printed in the United States of America

Published
by
Castle Top Group

FLYING MACHINES
SOCIAL MEDIA MODELERS REFERENCE MANUAL

GET CONNECTED WITH THIS BOOK

You can get connected online with us in the following ways

modelkitbook.com

facebook.com/themodelkitbook

modelkitbook@gmail.com

FLYING MACHINES
SOCIAL MEDIA MODELERS REFERENCE MANUAL

TABLE OF CONTENTS

Builder: Jezz Coleman

FLYING MACHINES
SOCIAL MEDIA MODELERS REFERENCE MANUAL

BUILDER LIST

Patrick "Paddy" Bryan
Jason Champion
Jezz Coleman
Snorre Sandviken
Phillipp Gruninger
Jay Blakemore (Jays Model Art)
Dawid Branski (Scale Hangar 182)
Ben Smith
Wayne Lawson
Gary Jewkes
Pouillard Christophe
Richard Spreckley
Ian Gaskell
Barry Koervers
Ashley Dunn
Donald Semora
Karen Easson
Andrew Root
Ivan Jensen Taylor
John Chestnut
Alex Green
Models For Heroes
Karl Tearney
Rene Van Der Hart
Alex Chambers
Dina Arzapalo
John Ashton

All attempts have been made to get the spelling of the builder correct.

FLYING MACHINES
SOCIAL MEDIA MODELERS REFERENCE MANUAL

DEDICATION

At the time of this book being published, the world was being ravaged by a deadly disease called Covid 19. As of the time of the publication of this book, over 880,000 people have died.

This reference book is dedicated to all of the first responders, Nurses, Doctors, police Fire, EMS and others who have in this very hard time still showed up to battle the deadly disease Covid-19

Your dedication and sacrifices made every single day are something that may not touch model builders all of the time. However, I know many builder friends who have families impacted by this deadly disease.

So Thank You All....

I also want to dedicate this book to every single person who helped with images, helped with suggestions on how to make it better, and who have supported this project. All of you both named within this book and not have been critical to its being what it is. Your generosity and your willingness to put up with my questions and more is so greatly appreciated.

This is truly a community online that is like no other.

Thank You all.

FLYING MACHINES
SOCIAL MEDIA MODELERS REFERENCE MANUAL

ABOUT THIS BOOK

Model building is at once a solitary hobby, but also one that brings strangers together in a way that not many hobbies do. We spend hours, days, weeks and even sometimes months working on a model kit. When it is done we sometimes enter them in contests, sometimes we just place them on a shelf to admire.

But since the advent of Social Media, there has become a new option. We snap some pictures of the build and place them proudly online for all to see. We get suggestions, feedback and learn that there are thousands like us. This once solitary hobby has now become one where we meet and engage with others next door, and also across the world even. Social Media has allowed all of us to talk in an instant to someone thousands of miles away. To learn from others in a way that is unique.

I am a very lucky person. I never even as recent as a few years ago ever could know the good men and women I would meet on Social Media. Strangers who become friends, even though we never have met face to face. To be entrusted with the privilege of doing these books. I know the honor that it is to see these builds, talk to these people. To be allowed to put the images of these wonderful builds into these books.

This book like all the ones previous to it, and the ones coming after it are my small attempt to showcase the average builder. The builder who does not have the contacts or the ability to get their work into modeling magazines, or other publications. I think everyone deserves a little praise. Some bit of gratitude for their hard work. Even when they do not ask for it.

This book is for all of you!

FLYING MACHINES
SOCIAL MEDIA MODELERS REFERENCE MANUAL

Reichenberg ReIV

Builder: Patrick "Paddy" Bryan

ABOUT THE BUILD

Builder:	Patrick "Paddy" Bryan
Manufacturer:	Bronco
Kit Type:	Reichenberg ReIV
Model Scale:	1:35
Builders Home:	United Kingdom

Fast Fact:

The Fieseler Fi 103R, code-named Reichenberg, was a late-World War II German crewed version of the V-1 flying bomb. The V-1 was transformed into the Reichenberg by adding a small, cramped cockpit at the point of the fuselage that was immediately ahead of the pulsejet's intake, where the standard V-1's compressed-air cylinders were fitted. The cockpit had basic flight instruments and a plywood bucket seat.

Me-109 e3

Builder: Jason Champion

The Builder Says:

This model is the weekend edition of the Eduard kit and has been built and is finished as German pilot and ace Josef Prillers aircraft from Summer 1940 used during the Battle of Britain. This was a straightforward build with a nice paint scheme to be able to practice mottling and free hand camouflage. The Paints that were used were RLM 65, 02, 04, 70 & 71 from the MRP paint range and the model weathering was done using various Ammo MiG panel liners, pigments and oil brushers.

ABOUT THE BUILD

Builder:	Jason Champion
Manufacturer:	Eduard
Kit Type:	Me-109 e3
Model Scale:	1:48
Builders Home:	United States

Me-109 e3

Builder: Jason Champion

Scan this QR Code and learn more about the maker of this model and his builds.

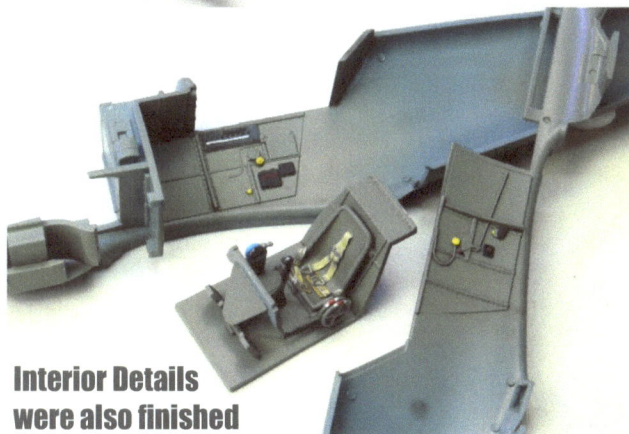

Fast Fact:

The German pilot that this model is based on Josef Priller flew 307 combat missions to claim 101 victories. All his victories were recorded over the Western Front, against British and American bombers and fighters.

Interior Details were also finished

Spitfire Mk 14

Builder: Jezz Coleman

Click here to go to the builders awesome Facebook group, where model builders from all over the world meet and talk builds.

Fast Fact:

The Spitfire Mk.XIV entered service with Nos. 91, 322 and 610 Squadrons in southeast England where it saw notable success as an interceptor against V-1 Flying Bombs but also as part of the 2nd Tactical Air Force in operations over occupied Europe. Spitfire Mk.XIVs were also planned The Spitfire Mk.XIV met mixed reviews from its pilots; whilst there was no doubt of the huge performance increase the new variant offered, it was uncomfortable to fly and lacked the balance and control harmonization of earlier Merlin engine Spitfires.

ABOUT THE BUILD

Builder:	Jezz Coleman
Manufacturer:	Airfix
Kit Type:	Spitfire Mk 14
Model Scale:	1:48
Builders Home:	United Kingdom

F.a2 Harrier

Builder: Jezz Coleman

The BAE Systems FA2 Sea Harrier fighter aircraft, which was in service with the British Royal Navy. It's role was air defence for the carrier fleet, particularly against low-flying attack aircraft armed with long range air-to-surface missiles. The FA2 first flew in 1988 and entered service in 1993. 56 aircraft were built for the Royal Navy. The Sea Harrier was retired from the UK Royal Navy in March 2006, but is currently in service with the Indian Navy.

ABOUT THE BUILD

Builder:	Jezz Coleman
Manufacturer:	Kinetic
Kit Type:	F.a2 Harrier
Model Scale:	1:35
Builders Home:	United Kingdom

SU-27

Builder: Snorre Sandviken

Model type: Su-27 Flanker
Converted into P-42 Streak
Flanker.

ABOUT THE BUILD

Builder:	Snorre Vandviken
Manufacturer:	Eduard / Adademy
Kit Type:	SU-27
Model Scale:	1:48
Builders Home:	Norway

Fast Fact:

This Aircraft was basically a stripped down SU-27 Flanker Russian Fighter. Between 1986 and 1988 the P-42, piloted variously by Victor Pugachev, Nikolai Sadovnikov, Oleg Tsoi and Yevgeni Frolov, took no less than 27 records from the Streak Eagle, including time to height records for 3000, 6000, 9000, 12000 and 15000 meters, and a height record of 19335m (63435 ft) and time-to-height records with various payloads. The aircraft even set records for STOL aircraft with a take-off run of less than 1540ft ! Most of these records still stand to this day.

Boeing Rc 135-S

Builder: Phillipp Gruninger

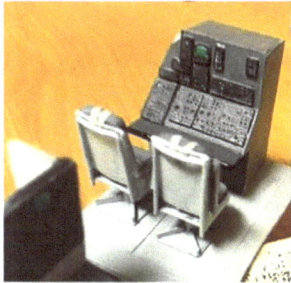

Interior Details were also finished

ABOUT THE BUILD

Builder:	Phillipp Gruninger
Manufacturer:	Revell
Kit Type:	Boeing RD-135-S
Model Scale:	1:48
Builders Home:	Germany

The Builder Says:

This project started as a 1/48 ID Models KC-135A vacu form kit i got from ebay. Lacking of any structural or surface detail, usable clear parts, decals & landing gear, i decided to do something totally different. After reading the story of RC-135S Rivet Ball a.k.a. Wanda Belle on King Hawes´ great site www.rc135.com, i fell in love with this plane and knew what to do. Since the original bird had ten huge circular windows on the starboard side, i had to build the interior, which includes nine cameras and optical sensors and the control panels and consoles, full cockpit, crew rest area, seats, kitchen corner, and the reconnaissance equipment and interior light in warm white and red for the Raven´s positions. All details like landing gear & wheels, clear parts, engine detail, radomes etc. is scratch-built. The whole airframe received rivets and panel lines, with oil canning effect on some spots. Electric power comes through a small plug in the wheel bay. The power source is connected through a 1/48 starter generator/power unit from Hasegawa. I included some crewmen, like the pilots and technicians from various kits, and modified them. The Manual Tracker dome on top of the fuselage came from a 1/48 Lockheed Ventura, half the main landing gear wheels from a 1/48 B-1, the other half is copied in FIMO. Interior is fully scratch-built from the Rest of the styrene sheet the kit was molded. Pilots seats were from a C-130, but heavily modified. Painting was done with Revell Enamel colors through the Airbrush as usual.

Fw-190 A4

Builder: Jay Blakemore - Jays Model Art

The Builder Says:

Eduard's new-tooled Fw190 series continues to grow at a tremendous pace since its debut release in 2017. The initial offering, and the subject of this build, featured the A-4 variant, though most types can now be modeled with the alternative wing and fuselage parts provided in the more than ten boxings now available, including an awesome Royal Class release. The styrene parts assemble effortlessly, though if it is your wish to complicate things, there are resin engines, gun-bays, cockpits and underwing stores available in Eduard's Brassin accessory range, some of which have been used here.

ABOUT THE BUILD

Builder:	Jay Blakemore
Manufacturer:	Eduard
Kit Type:	Fw 190
Model Scale:	1:48
Builders Home:	United Kingdom

Fw-190 A-4

Builder: Jay Blakemore - Jays Model Art

ABOUT:

Self-taught, British born airbrush artist & modeller Jay Blakemore, works from his village-based studio situated in the heart of England.

Click the QR Code to go to the builders portfolio of other builds

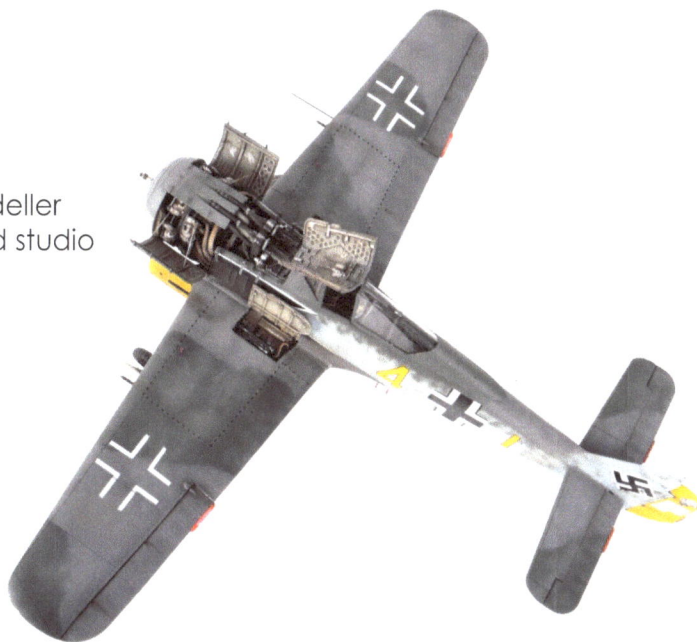

ABOUT THE BUILD

Builder:	Dawid Branski
Manufacturer:	Revell
Kit Type:	Junkers Ju-52
Model Scale:	1:48
Builders Home:	United Kingdom

When Adolf Hitler was elected chancellor of Germany in 1933, he realizing the importance of a strong airforce, he instructed the Air Ministry to put a plan into action to build a 1,000-plane air force. He did this despite the fact that Germany was prohibited from having any military type aircraft due to the Treaty of Versailles. Rather than develop an entirely new transport aircraft, the ministry ordered the immediate but discreet conversion of a large number of existing various aircraft from civilian use to military use.

They selected the Ju-52, and this was done as minimal alteration was needed to convert it for military use. The Ju-52/3m freight version had a hatch in the roof for loading by crane, a large cargo door on the starboard side just behind the wing, and a door for passengers on the port side. A new hole was cut into the roof to accommodate a dorsal machine gun, and the interior was reconfigured for different missions.

Fast Fact:

First Flight:	**October 13, 1930**
Manufacturer:	**Junkers**
Designer:	**Ernst Zindel**

COVER AIRCRAFT

Junkers JU-52

Builder: Dawid Branski

Fast Fact:

This WWII Aircraft was nicknamed Tante Ju, which is German for Aunt Ju, it was also known as "Iron Annie" as it was a very sturdy and reliable aircraft.

Revell

LEVEL 5

1:48

❖ 170 PARTS
↔ 39,3 cm
↕ 61,5 cm

NEW

JUNKERS
Ju52/3mg4e TRANSPORT

Currenent Box art, however this kit has been through several reboxings in its lifetime.

The detail level on this kit is shown here, in the flaps that can be built adjusted to the way the builder wants them.

Junkers JU-52 🇬🇧

COVER AIRCRAFT

Builder: Dawid Branski

This builder has a popular YouTube channel where he showcases and features various models, and model builds. Link to this channel is on the next page.

One of the biggest issues with the kit are the delicate wing flaps, and most all build blogs do suggest you place these as late in the build as possible.

COVER AIRCRAFT

Junkers JU-52

Builder: Dawid Branski

With at the time of the making of this book over 83K subscribers and 6 million views on his videos, click on the QR code to the right to check out the builders YouTube channel.

Fast Fact:

These aircraft were also used for mine hunting in water. The Aircraft was fitted with a large Dural hoop braced beneath the wing and fuselage. This hoop was than energised by an additional motor that was installed in the fuselage. The magnetic field that was generated that way, triggered magnetically fused mines.

F4 Phantom Fgr.2

Builder: Ben Smith

ABOUT THE BUILD

Builder:	Ben Smith
Manufacturer:	Airfix
Kit Type:	F4 Phantom Fgr.2
Model Scale:	1:72
Builders Home:	United Kingdom

The Builder Says:

Normally modern Aircraft are not my thing but for some reason I always liked the look of the Phantom in its RAF Camouflage and loaded to the teeth with ordnance. So when Airfix released its FGR2 I knew I had to build it. The kit itself is nicely appointed with plenty of options through out the build to enable the builder to build the aircraft in various configurations. The detail is nice throughout and the kit builds up nicely and is well engineered to minimize the work required on seams.

The most daunting phase of any phantom build is the amount of decals. There is hundreds. Time and patience is required (two weeks of evening decal sessions) but it's well worth the effort as the whole kit builds into a really pleasing model of the Phantom FGR.2

F4 Phantom Fgr.2

Builder: Ben Smith

Remember that decal comment? Well, take a look. Time and a lot of patience is needed when doing these on this kind of model.

This model is one of the most decal heavy models you can buy. There are literally hundreds of small decals that need to be placed. This is why this model is one fo the models that some builders avoid. However once done, they are one of the mode impressive models you can display.

AV-8B Harrier

Builder: Wayne Lawson

The Builder Says:

The Harrier is the Hobbyboss 1/18 scale AV-8B Harrier II, built from the box (quiet literally we only got a table that I can use about a month ago) with no add ons or extras, painted with Vallejo paints, MIG lucky gloss varnish and Flory washes for weathering and panel lines.

ABOUT THE BUILD

Builder:	Wayne Lawson
Manufacturer:	Hobby Boss
Kit Type:	AV-8B Harrier
Model Scale:	1:18
Builders Home:	United Kingdom

Fast Fact:

The Harrier was designed and first flew two years before we put a man on the moon. The aircraft is subsonic and can hover according to some at up to 5,000 feet.

Mosquito M4

Builder: Gary Jewkes

The Builder:

The builder has been back in the hobby nor for about a year and before that had not been building models since he was 13. Gary is from the U.K. and he did this as a group build to do with British Bombers. His main interest is 1/48 scale D-Day based aircraft.

ABOUT THE BUILD

Builder:	Gary Jewkes
Manufacturer:	Tamiya
Kit Type:	Mosquito M4
Model Scale:	1:72
Builders Home:	United Kingdom

Super Sea Sprite

Builder: Pouillard Christophe

Fast Fact:

The UH-2 was introduced in time to see action in the Tonkin Gulf incident in August 1964. The Seasprite's principal contribution , was the retrieval of downed aircrews.

ABOUT THE BUILD

Builder:	Pouillard Christophe
Manufacturer:	Kitty Hawk
Kit Type:	Super Seasprite
Model Scale:	1:48
Builders Home:	Belgium

Super Sea Sprite
Builder: Pouillard Christophe

One of the plusses of this kit is that Kitty Hawk includes some photo-etch in the kit. So this will help the builder add various details to the kit if they wish. Photo-Etch is becoming more and more standard in kits.

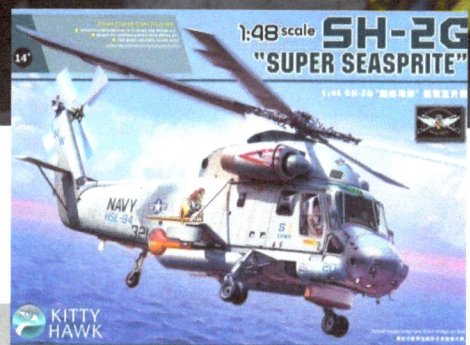

Kitty Hawk Box Art

Different model builders, do different things to make their models stand out. Sometimes it is aftermarket parts. However sometimes it is the scratch built small thing that set off the model.

Here the builder placed a pilots map on the the instrument panel dash. Something small and maybe even this will not be seen by the person looking at the model. However it is the small things like this that can make a nice model a awesome model.

A-6A Intruder

Builder: Richard Spreckley

The Builder Says:

This particular build is inspired from one of Richards all-time favourite films 'Flight of the Intruder': Using the HobbyBoss quarter scale kit of the Grumman A6E (TRAM) Intruder to build a marque that was used to evaluate an experimental camouflage scheme on the USS Constellation in February 1990. The A6 Intruder was designed as an all weather medium attack aircraft to replace the Douglas Skyraider. The A6 had a unique capability at subsonic speeds, as it was an extremely stable platform that could carry a considerable payload, whilst still maintaining excellent manoeuverability

ABOUT THE BUILD

Builder:	Richard Spreckley
Manufacturer:	Hobby Boss
Kit Type:	A6E Intruder
Model Scale:	1:48
Builders Home:	United Kingdom

A-6A Intruder

Builder: Richard Spreckley

The Build:

This kit is extremely forgiving as it allows many elements to be built in a modular fashion. This really does help when it comes to the detailed painting and weathering later down the line. The Aires resin cockpit is actually designed for the Revell kit, to get it to fit correctly there is a requirement for plenty of test fitting and removal of excess resin. Surprisingly the only issue that caused me concern was the front bulkhead, which has to be able to accept the radar bulkhead within a very tight space. Considering this is a complex build the majority of the kit went together very nicely. The area which did take some time, and putty was the lower fuselage where it joined the nose and engine nacelles. All the separate parts that had been built were primed with a UMP light grey primer before gull grey by Vallejo air for the cockpit, and white for most of the other parts, including the undercarriage system and engine intakes. Any metal colours were first primed with Vallejo metal gloss black before adding the appropriate colours: In this case the engines were done in Vallejo metal's Duraluminium. Detailing was hand painted using white, yellow and red for the cockpit. Once all the subsections had been painted then the main assembly began. The cockpit fitted nicely into the fuselage, with only a small amount of fettling required around the front nose section. What was a slight disappointment was the windshield, which had clearly warped and needed re-shaping using a cocktail stick to widen the base of the windshield. What was really impressive was the ingenious method of supporting the weight of the aircraft on metal landing gear which was encased in plastic mouldings. Standard Mk 82 bombs were then selected for the maximum look on the final build.

A-6A Intruder

Builder: Richard Spreckley

The Model On Its Presentation Stand

Hobby Boss has produced one of the best kits on the market depicting the A6 Intruder. Being a US Navy aircraft it is a complex shape and design which has been beautifully replicated by HB. What is really impressive are the metal undercarriage supports which are used with detailed plastic sleeves to produce very realistic landing gear. The kit also gives the builder the option of wings folded or not, and all the control surfaces can be fully or partially extended or retracted. It also provides an option for the nose to be open with the main radar exposed.

The amount of ordnance supplied in the kit allows several different configurations to be used. Some modellers use tiny magnets so that the load outs can be changed, however in this case a more traditional approach was used. The cockpit is nicely appointed and for an out of the box build would provide any finished model with a great looking 'office'. However due to the 'greenhouse' nature of the A6, Aires's resin cockpit was used as it gives far more detail than the kit version. HobbyBoss provides decals for two aircraft: the more traditional scheme from the VA-75 'Sunday Punchers' on the USS John F Kennedy or the more unusual half desert camouflage scheme from VA-65 'The World Famous Fighting Tigers' on the USS Theodore Roosevelt. To replicate the green camouflage scheme from VA-165 the decal sheet produced by Fightertown decals was used as a template.

A26 Invader

Builder: Ian Gaskell

ABOUT THE BUILD

Builder:	Ian Gaskell
Manufacturer:	ICM
Kit Type:	A-26 Counter Invader
Model Scale:	1:48
Builders Home:	United Kingdom

The Builder Says:

My completed 1/48 ICM A-26K Counter Invader, converted from their B-26B-50 kit. Aftermarket used: -Cutting Edge A-26K resin conversion set (meant for the old Monogram/Revell kit). Eduard bombs and rocket pods and launchers. Aero Master decal set. Model Master metal gun barrels. Quickboost resin seats. Part scratchbuilt cockpit. EZ Line. Hataka Orange Line Vietnam paint set.

Fast Fact:

The Counter Invader was a highly modified version of the Douglas A-26 Invader, a World War II attack bomber. Redesignated B-26 in 1948, the Invader served again during the Korean War (1950-1953), mainly as a night intruder against North Korean supply lines. It was removed from service in 1958

Mig 25 RBT

Builder: Barry Koervers

ABOUT THE BUILDS

Builder:	Barry Koervers
Manufacturer:	ICM
Kit Type:	Mig 25RBT Foxbat
Model Scale:	1/72
Builders Home:	Scotland

The Builder Says:

I really enjoyed building the Foxbat, the engineering is very good and I am lead to believe that this is simply a scaled down version of the excellent 48th scale Foxbat which I also have in my stash. The details are great out of the box but there are various after market sets if you want to go to the next level, however I was satisfied and it was a very quick build that was achieved over a couple of weeks.

Mig 25 RBT

Builder: Barry Koervers

Fast Fact:

Paints Used to Finish

- MRP Traffic Grey
- MRP MiG-31 Chassis Covers
- MRP Black
- MRP Tire Black
- MRP Russian Wheel Green
- MRP Russian Cockpit Green
- AK Xtreme Metal Aluminium
- AK Xtreme Metal Burnt Metal
- AK Xtreme Metal Purple
- AK Xtreme Metal Blue

Misc Builds

Builder: Ashley Dunn

Hobby Boss 1/48 A-10 Thunderbolt

Kinetic 1/48 Kfir C.1

ABOUT THE BUILDS

Builder:	Ashley Dunn
Manufacturer:	Various
Kit Type:	Various
Model Scale:	Various
Builders Home:	Scotland

Kinetic 1/48 CF-18 Hornet

Fast Fact:

The name Huckebein is a reference to a trouble-making raven from an illustrated story in 1867 by Wilhelm Busch

Academy 1/48 TA-183 Huckebien

Hellcat

Builder: Jezz Coleman

ABOUT THE BUILD

Builder: Jezz Coleman

Manufacturer: Eduard

Kit Type: Hellcat

Model Scale: 1:48

Builders Home: United Kingdom

The Builder Says:

Eduard Weekend Editions ProfiPack boxings include lots of very finely detailed photo-etched parts, and sometimes a vast selection of decals with multiple color and marking schemes, with well illustrated instruction booklets. However, the Weekend editions are a no nonsense, no added frills, standard model kit. And with that in mind I intended to do as the kit said build it in a weekend.

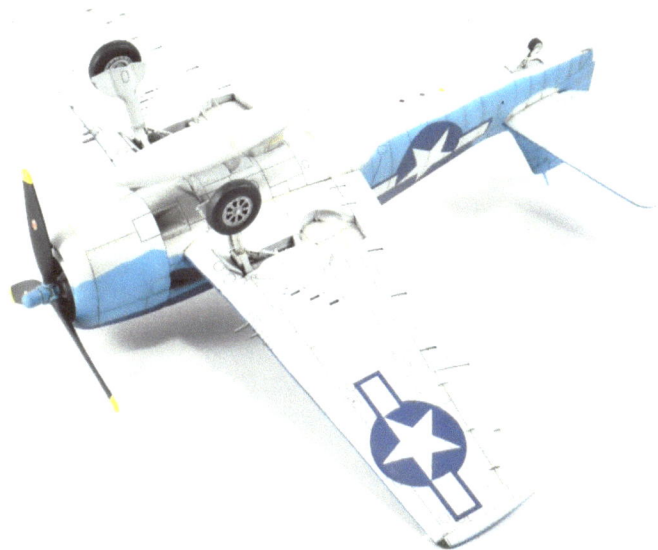

Aliens Dropship

Builder: Donald Semora

BUILT BY

Ds

DONALD SEMORA

**Click the QR Code
to go to the builders
portfolio of other builds**

The Builder Says:

This is a long out of production resin cast model of what is an iconic subject. The Colonial Marines Dropship from the movie Aliens. What was nice about this kit was the ease of assembly and the cool subject. There has only been one other model of this type made, and that was by Halcyon. Those kits stopped production very fast in the 80's due to Trademark issues. This kit was a licensed model by 20th Century Fox.

Aliens Dropship

Builder: Donald Semora

Fast Fact:

Several dropship props were built for filming, starting with a six-foot model on which all of the other miniatures were based. Most of the dropship miniatures were constructed from fiberglass, the majority were stunt versions. Only one miniature featured motorized weapons pods and landing gear.

ABOUT THE BUILD

Builder:	Donald Semora
Manufacturer:	Protos Games
Kit Type:	Aliens Dropship
Model Scale:	1:48
Builders Home:	United States

Builders Opinion:

In August of 2016 Prodos Games made an announcement on their site that they were releasing the Dropship. Their idea was to make each model to order, and to hone in on how each would be unique.

However in the end this I think backfired on them as almost immediately after they began selling the models, there were complaints of long wait times for models, and casting issues. Compounding the confusion was that Prodos had two places listed that they operated out of. The United Kindgom and Poland. Where the models were made I think was Poland, the first one I ordered came from there, and it took 9 weeks. So soon the company I think phased them out. They are still listed on their site, however there are no links to be able to buy one. I think if they made them in batches of 10 or 20 and sold them based off of that, they would be enjoying better results. I hope to see them ramp up the making of these again soon.

Hawker Typhoon

Builder: Jason Champion

The Builder Says:

I love the scale and detail of this kit. I finished it almost Out of the box, With resin seat, wheels and aftermarket rockets the only additions.

Historical Fact:

ABOUT THE BUILD

Builder:	Jason Champion
Manufacturer:	Airfix
Kit Type:	Hawker Typhoon
Model Scale:	1:24
Builders Home:	United Kingdom

Sergeant A. Shannon of No. 257 Squadron reported, "I remember the Typhoon as being a hairy machine, and the wind would put you up long before you ever met it…. The engine was quite a huge thing … and frightened the life out of me when I just got in and opened the throttle. I felt, after the takeoff which didn't disturb me too much, that I was up to 15,000 feet before I knew it—before I started to think! It was frightening, and I rather think it flew me rather than I flew it, for a while."

Fw 190 D-9

Builder: Karen Easson

ABOUT THE BUILD

Builder:	Karen Easson
Manufacturer:	Eduard
Kit Type:	Fw 190 D9
Model Scale:	1:48
Builders Home:	United States

The Builder Says:

The kits used in the dio was Eduard 1/48 FW 190 D-9 and Tamyia 1/48 Luftwaffe winter crew with kettenrad. The base is on a thin wood board, coated with sand and wood glue, added pencils shavings to simulate dead grass and leaves and used deluxe's scenic snow for a lightly snowy look. Some minor scratch building on the tank and the airbrush, there was no connection to the 2 so I used tubing that was around some old wire I had for that and attached one end to the tank and the other to the bottom of the airbrush. On the sentry guard there was no strap on his weapon so made one out of Tamyia tape and painted it. The antenna on the FW was done with guitar string. All else was pretty much OOB.

JU-87 Stuka 🇬🇧

Builder: Jay Blakemore - Jays Model Art

Click the QR Code to go to the site of this builder and learn more about their work.

ABOUT THE BUILD

Builder:	Jay Blakemore
Manufacturer:	Airfix
Kit Type:	Stuka
Model Scale:	1:48
Builders Home:	United Kingdom

F-14 Tomcat
Builder: Dawid Branski

This builder has a popular YouTube channel where he showcases and features various models, and model builds. Click the QR code to go to his channel and check out his builds.

ABOUT THE BUILD

Builder:	Dawid Branski
Manufacturer:	Fine Molds
Kit Type:	F-14 Tomcat
Model Scale:	1:72
Builders Home:	United Kingdom

Felixestow F.2

Builder: Andrew Root

ABOUT THE BUILD

Builder:	Andrew Root
Manufacturer:	Wingnut Wings
Kit Type:	Felixstowe
Model Scale:	1:32
Builders Home:	United Kingdom

Fast Fact:

With a crew of five and a flying time of 10 hours, this aircraft was used as an observation plane, however also it was used to hunt zeppelins and Uboats.

Felixestow F.1
Builder: Andrew Root

According to the manufacturers website, the kit Includes 2 models; 1x Felixstowe F.2a (91cm x 44cm) & 1x Hansa-Brandenburg W.29 (42cm x 29cm) - 2 high quality Cartograf decal sheets with markings for Felixstowe F.2a N4305 & Hansa-Brandenburg W.29 2512 including naval hexagon camouflage - 590 high quality injection moulded plastic parts - Beaching dollies and trestles - Highly detailed 375hp Rolls Royce Eagle VIII and 150hp Benz Bz.III engines Metal wing spar (W.29) - 55 photo-etched metal detail parts - Fine in scale rib tape detail – Full rigging diagrams - Almost no rigging required for the W.29

Wingnut Wings Box Art

Nakajima Ki-43

Builder: Ivan Jensen Taylor

Fast Fact:

During WWII, most pilots who encountered this aircraft and called them Zeros, however most of these so-called Zeros were actually this aircraft, the Nakajima Ki-43. Known as the Army Zero and later code named "Oscar,"

The Ki-43 became the most important Japanese Imperial Air Force fighter of World War II. With its inline radial engine, light weight and speed. Early in the war it was by far one of the best fighters of WWII. But the downside to the aircraft early on, was that it did not have armor for the pilot, nor self sealing fuel tanks, so allied pilots would report that although they were hard to hit and nimble, they did burn easy once hit.

This aircraft became one of the workhorses of the suicide missions Japanese engaged in known as Kamikaze.

ABOUT THE BUILD

Builder:	Ivan Jensen Taylor
Manufacturer:	Hasagawa
Kit Type:	Nakajima Ki-43
Model Scale:	1:48
Builders Home:	United Kingdom

Polikarpov I-153

Builder: Ivan Jensen Taylor

ICM Box Art

ABOUT THE BUILD

Builder:	Ivan Jensen Taylor
Manufacturer:	ICM
Kit Type:	Polikarpov I-153
Model Scale:	1:32
Builders Home:	United Kingdom

This links to the builders Facebook page, where he showcases all of his work.

F3H Demon

Builder: Jezz Coleman

Build Blog

Please note that images are of the build, and may not be exactly relating to the article point.

The McDonnell F3H Demon is another of the airplanes that doesn't get the respect that it deserves from the aviation enthusiast. For this build I decided to to use a 1/72 offering from sword models, being the first short-run kit I have built I entered into this with an open mind as I have heard it through the grapevine that they may well not be a shake and bake kit.

On opening the kit you are presented with several grey sprues with the addition of a resin exhaust along with two optional ejector seats, and a small sheet of P/E.

ABOUT THE BUILD

Builder:	Jezz Coleman
Manufacturer:	Sword Models
Kit Type:	F3H Demon
Model Scale:	1:72
Builders Home:	United Kingdom

After examining all of the parts it was on with the build which I thought look quite straightforward however this aircraft certainly lived up to its namesake throughout the whole build. Build started with the cockpit, the details here were average to say the least but workable in such a small scale once it was painted up in its respective colors.

Authors note here: As you can see the builder undercoats in black, that way when he paints the base coat the stippling in the fine recesses happens. This give any model depth and eye appeal.

F3H Demon

Builder: Jezz Coleman

The saving grace was the addition of the resin ejection seat painted up and uninstalled which added some interest to the area. This was then glued into position between the forward fuselage pieces, it was then on to the rear section of the fuselage there was a small engine outlet to be glued into the rear of the fuselage before the two halves we've brought together following that the front and rear portions of the fuselage needed bring in together however this is Where I encountered one of my first issues the front portion was too large to fit into the bulkhead of the rear fuselage section. With some careful sanding and numerous test fitting I managed to get a reasonable fit

Next step was to glue the upper and lower portions of the wings together. Presenting me with My next challenge attaching them to the fuselage. The design of the wing attachment was rather unusual it literally just butt jointed to the side of the fuselage with just one locating pin to align two wings on each side, much to my surprise the join of the wing root was quite good so with various tape and elastic bands holding everything in place to dry fully before moving on this was left overnight for the glue to set.

F3H Demon

Builder: Jezz Coleman

Build Blog
Please note that images are of the build, and may not be exactly relating to the article point.

Fast Fact:

Due to excellent visibility from the cockpit, the Demon earned the nickname "The Chair". Demon pilots were known colloquially as "Demon Drivers" and those who worked on the aircraft were known as "Demon Doctors". The unfavorable power-to-weight ratio gave rise to the less flattering nickname "lead sled", sometimes shortened to "sled"

Using some sanding pads I cleaned up the seams and rescribed any details that were lost during this process. Then I added some of the P/E (airbrakes and fins to the wings) the smaller components such as the undercarriage legs and doors required a small amount of clean up to remove some flash and it was ready for painting along with the fuselage. With the canopy also masked I then applied a coat of matt black primer to everything.

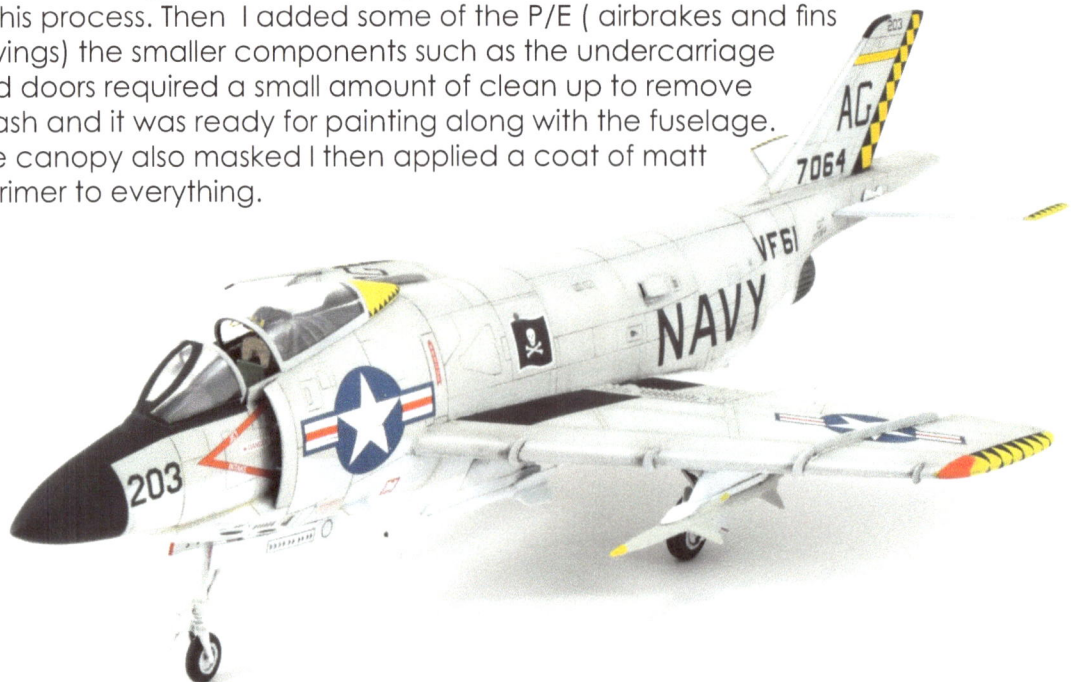

F3H Demon

Builder: Jezz Coleman

Click here to go to the builders awesome Facebook group, where model builders from all over the world meet and talk builds.

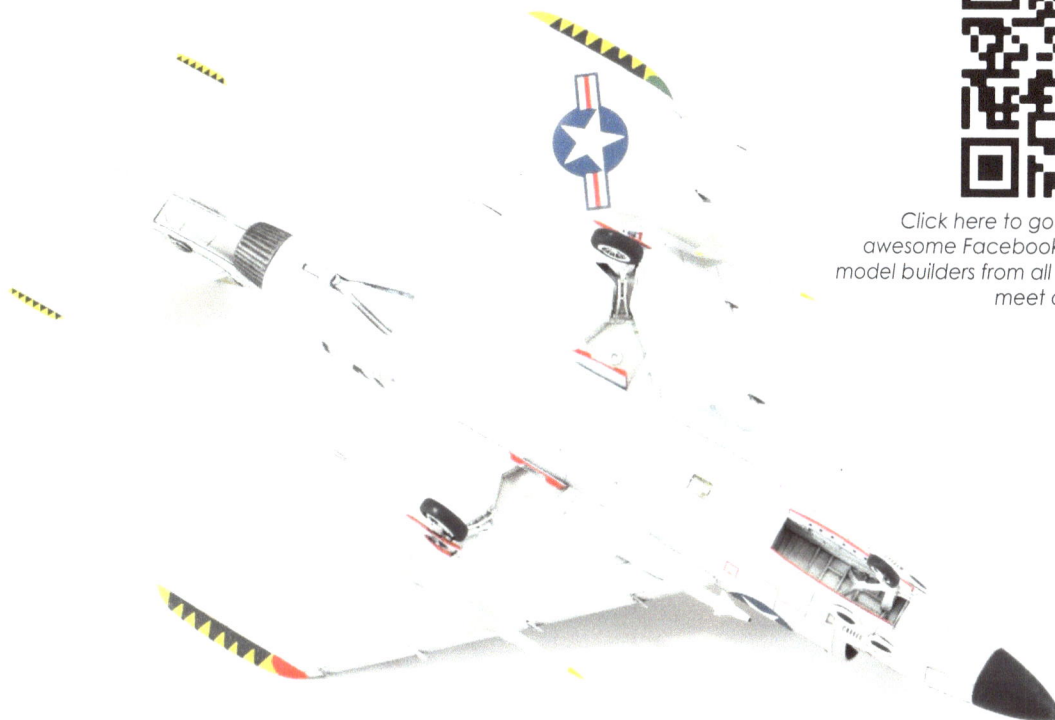

The Underside of the aircraft was airbrushed using Hataka Traffic White this was then masked of using blue tac sausages and the upper area was painted with Hataka paints, and some post shading was applied using a lighter shade of the base color to add some tonal difference. The various areas of the fuselage were masked off and painted as per the instructions a clear coat was added to all the components prior to decals which went on and conformed nice, the only problem i encountered with the decals was sword had not printed the correct amount of wingtip decals meaning i had ro raid the spares box for some black strips of decal paper and cut my own out and apply. With all the decals finally added and given another coat of clear I added a oil pin wash to the panel lines and also added some additional weathering streaking etc. All that was left to do was to glue the in place all the smaller details such as the undercarriage legs, gear bay doors, canopy refueling probe etc.

Last but not least i gave the entire model a coat of matt varnish to seal it all final thing was to remove the masking from the canopy and I was calling this build done.

I am over all pleased with how it came out in the end. However here comes the BUT...

F3H Demon

Builder: Jezz Coleman

Build Blog

Please note that images are of the build, and may
not be exactly relating to the article point.

The finished model on display

This build fought me almost every step of the way and tried my patience at times. i put it down
and walked away at times. But i was not going to let myself be defeated i can now say ive built
a short run kit but believe me when i say i will not be rushing to do another to soon.

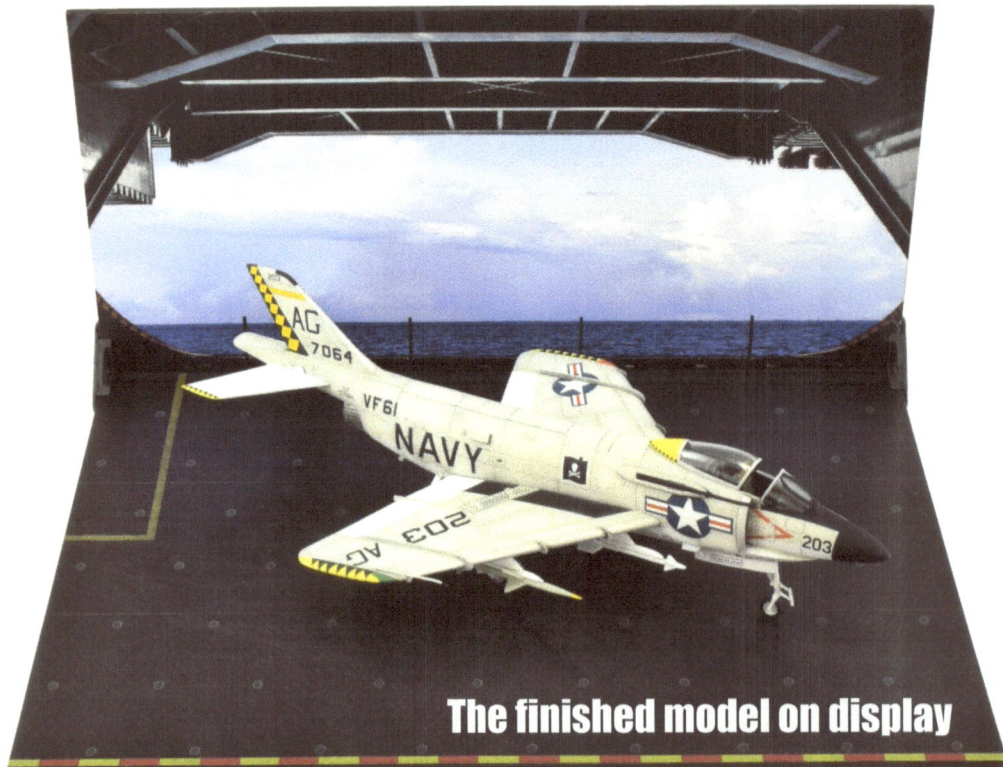

The finished model on display

Polikarpov I-16

Builder: Snorre Sandviken

ABOUT THE BUILD

Builder:	Snorre Sandviken
Manufacturer:	ICM
Kit Type:	Polikarpov I-16
Model Scale:	1:32
Builders Home:	Norway

Fast Fact:

The pilots nicknamed the aircraft Ishak Russian for Donkey / Hinny.

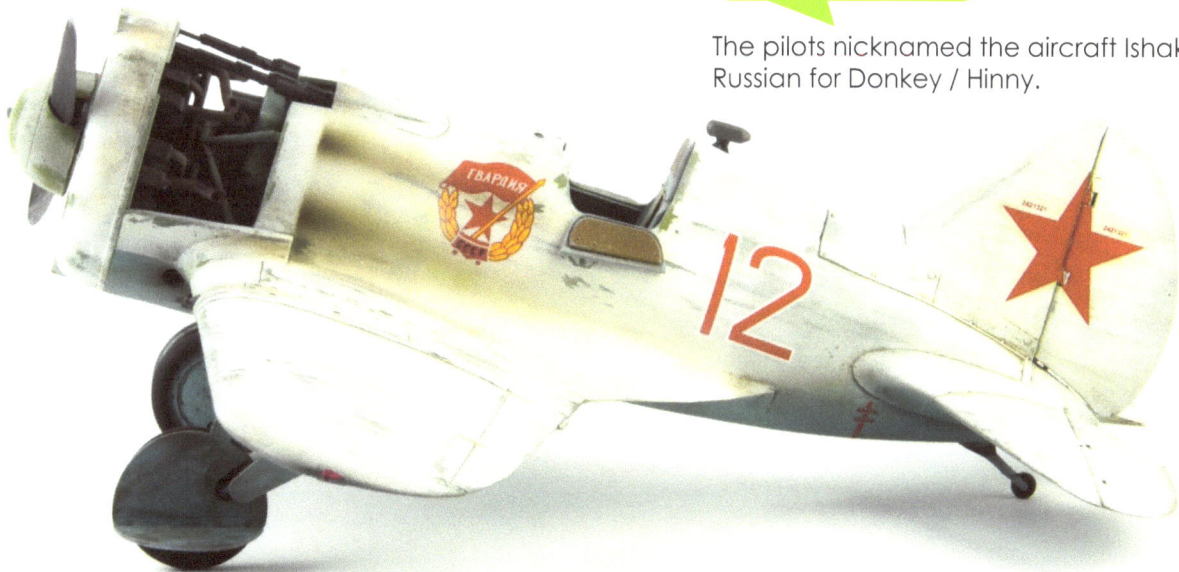

Jedi Starfighter

Builder: John Chestnut

ABOUT THE BUILD

Builder:	John Chestnut
Manufacturer:	AMC - ERTL
Kit Type:	Jedi Starfighter
Model Scale:	1:58
Builders Home:	United States

Fast Fact:

Lucas films made this model for the second trilogy of films, and it was designed to be the main fighter for the Jedi. Several kit makers have put out versions of this model. However the ICM/ERTL version is the most popular among builders, for its detail.

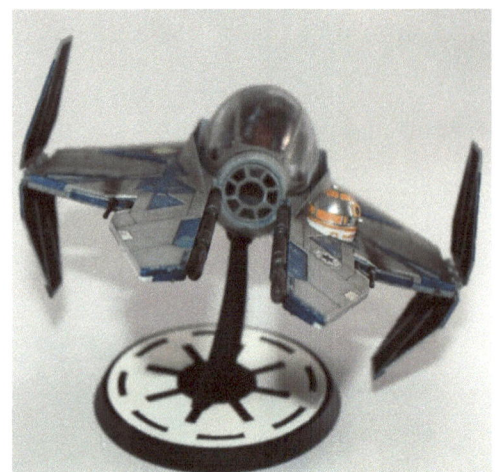

F104 J Starfighter

Builder: John Chestnut

Fast Fact:

The Starfighter featured a radical wing design, with thin, stubby wings attached substantially farther back on the fuselage than most of its contemporary aircraft. The wing provided excellent supersonic and high-speed, low-altitude aircraft performance, but resulted in poor turning capability and high landing speeds. It was the first production aircraft to achieve Mach 2, and the first aircraft to reach an altitude of 100,000 feet after taking off under its own power. The F104 Starfighter established world records for airspeed, altitude, and time to climb in 1958, becoming the first aircraft to hold all three simultaneously. It was also the first aircraft to be equipped with the powerful M61 Vulcan auto cannon and the AIM-9 Sidewinder missile.

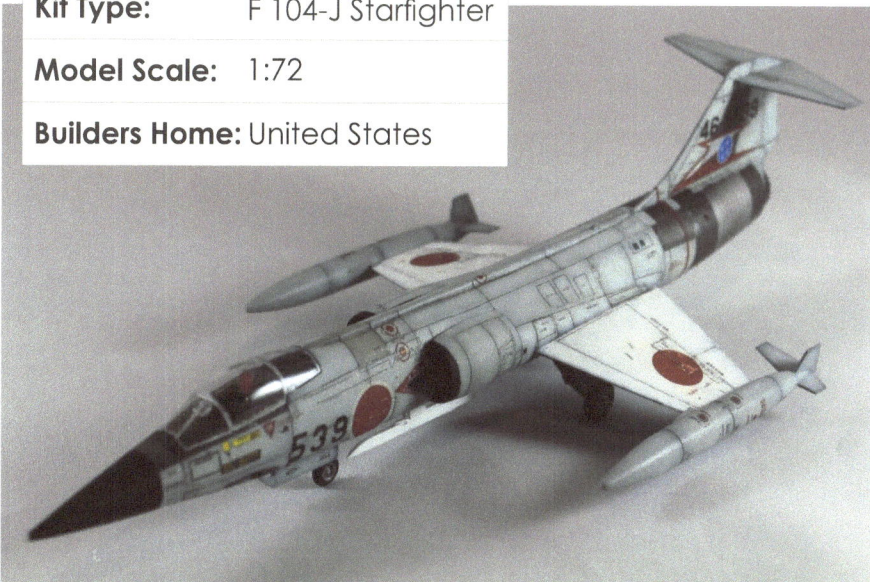

ABOUT THE BUILD

Builder:	John Chestnut
Manufacturer:	Hasagawa
Kit Type:	F 104-J Starfighter
Model Scale:	1:72
Builders Home:	United States

Model Markings:

This model was built to show the markings for the F-104's that served the Japanese airforce.

Tempest Mk. V 🇬🇧

Builder: Ivan Jensen Taylor

ABOUT THE BUILD

Builder:	Ivan Jensen Taylor
Manufacturer:	Special Hobby
Kit Type:	Hawker Tempest Mk. V
Model Scale:	1:32
Builders Home:	United Kingdom

This links to the builders Facebook page, where he showcases all of his work.

Japanese Zero

Builder: Pouillard Christophe

The level of detail places into this model is amazing. The little things do make a huge difference. Subtle things like the instrument details, and the pin washing to show the rivets etc. From average to amazing.

ABOUT THE BUILD

Builder: Pouillard Christophe

Manufacturer: Tamiya

Kit Type: Japanese Zero

Model Scale: 1:32

Builders Home: Belgium

T28C TROJAN

Builder: Pouillard Christophe

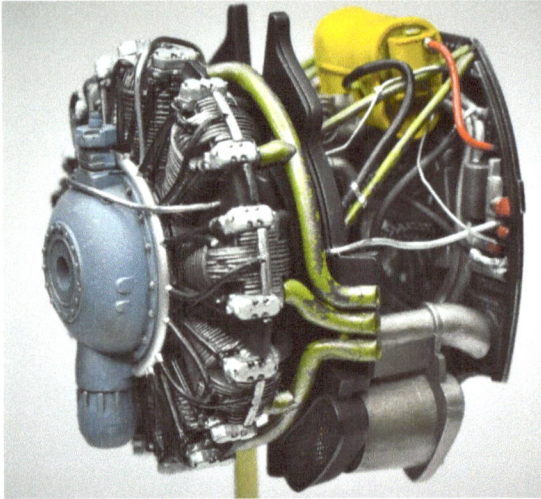

ABOUT THE BUILD

Builder:	Pouillard Christophe
Manufacturer:	Kitty Hawk
Kit Type:	T-28C Trojan
Model Scale:	1:32
Builders Home:	Belgium

F104 Egg Plane

Builder: Jezz Coleman

One of the interesting things about this kit, is that it is more detailed, with more accesory parts than other "egg" planes of it's type. Thus the model I think would appeal to a more broader builder audience. A few examples is a pilot figure, and missiles etc.

Freedom Models Box Art

ABOUT THE BUILD

Builder:	Jezz Coleman
Manufacturer:	Freedom
Kit Type:	F-107
Model Scale:	Special
Builders Home:	Great Britain

Click here to go to the builders awesome Facebook group, where model builders from all over the world meet and talk builds.

P-39Q Airacobra

Builder: Dawid Branski

ABOUT THE BUILD

Builder:	Dawid Branski
Manufacturer:	Eduard
Kit Type:	P-39Q Airacobra
Model Scale:	1:48
Builders Home:	United Kingdom

Fast Fact:

The XP-39 made its maiden flight on 6 April 1938 at Wright Field, Ohio, achieving 390 mph (630 km/h) at 20,000 ft (6,100 m), reaching this altitude in only five minutes. However, the XP-39 was found to be short on performance at altitude. Flight testing had found its top speed at 20,000 feet to be lower than the 400 mph claimed in the original proposal.

Su-22 M4

Builder: Snorre Sandviken

Fast Fact:

The Su22 M4 was a Russian-French upgrade package offered for existing aircraft with modernized cockpit, HOTAS, improved avionic systems, and laser range finder replaced by Phazotron Thomson CSF radar.

The turquoise color of the Russian cockpit is a point of heavy contention sometimes in model groups. However, in reality any shade works, as old Societ union cockpits were painted with what would be called at best slightly inconsistent colors.

ABOUT THE BUILD

Builder:	Snorre Sandviken
Manufacturer:	Hobby Boss
Kit Type:	Su-22 M4
Model Scale:	1:48
Builders Home:	Norway

Millennium Falcon

Builder: Donald Semora

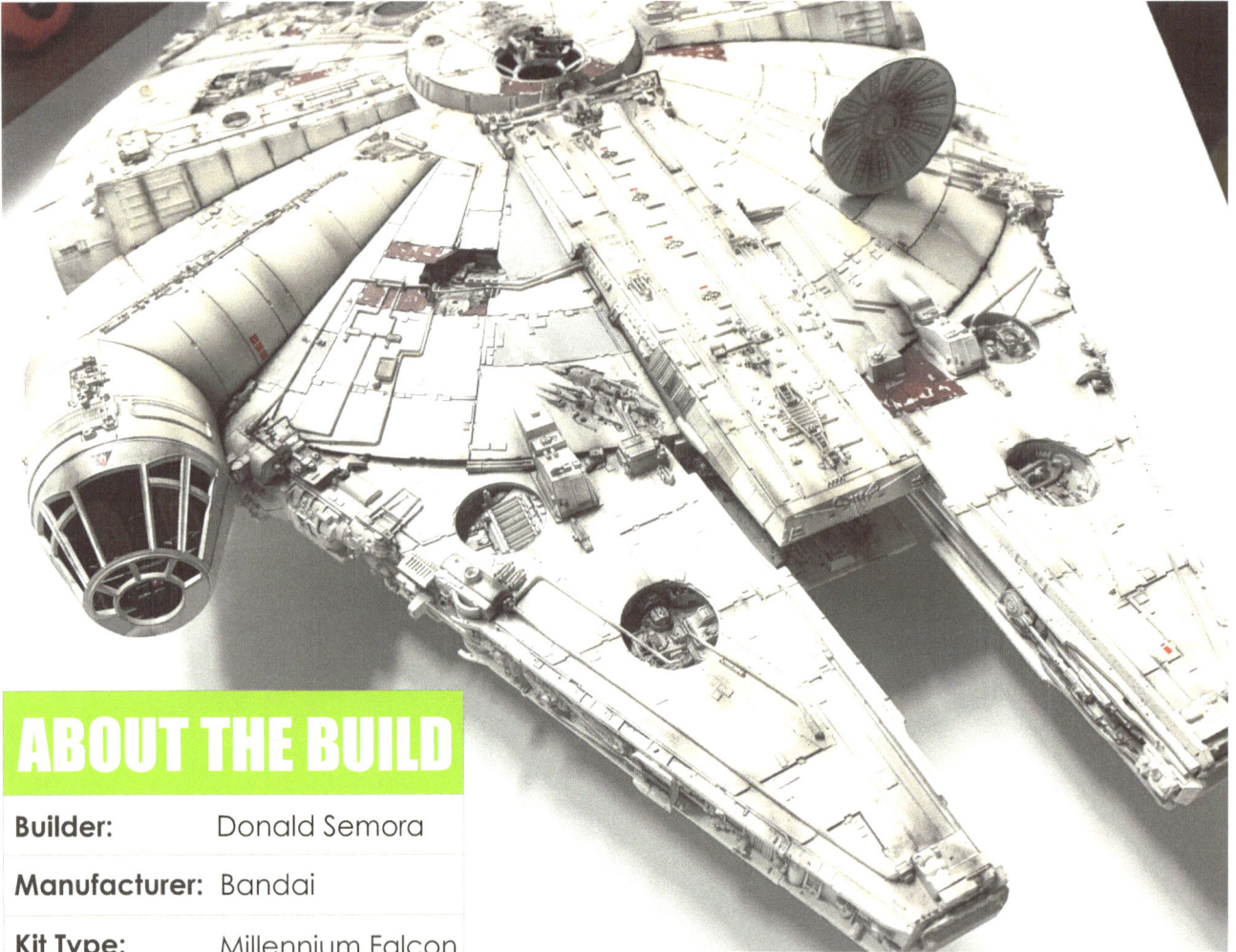

ABOUT THE BUILD

Builder:	Donald Semora
Manufacturer:	Bandai
Kit Type:	Millennium Falcon
Model Scale:	1:72
Builders Home:	United States

The Builder Says:

One thing I do, to mark a model as mine is with this model, I always use a metallic blue paint in the engine fan intakes. I think this adds a nice look, but also is a way I mark it as built by me.

BUILT BY

Ds

DONALD SEMORA

Millennium Falcon

Builder: Donald Semora

The Builder Says:

One of the biggest mistakes a builder can make when building this kit is to follow one of the most basic instructions. This is, that you do not need to glue pieces in place.

The model is a click -- Fit kit yes, however due to so many small pieces, you should use glue. Since I began making these models, and I have made over 30 of them, I learned the hard way, to use glue. Bandai did an awesome job on the overall engineering of the kit, and the pieces truly do fit literally perfectly together. However, some need to be rather firmly pressed into place, and if you do not do it right, they can and sometimes will fall out.

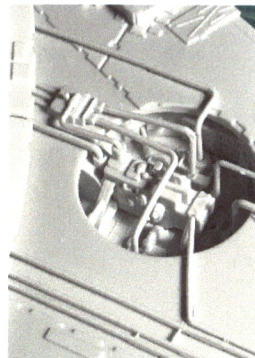

The detail level on this model kit is second to none.

Blackhawk

Builder: Karen Easson

ABOUT THE BUILD

Builder:	Karen Easson
Manufacturer:	Mini Craft
Kit Type:	Blackhawk
Model Scale:	1:48
Builders Home:	United States

Fast Fact:

The HH-60M MEDEVAC helicopter integrates advanced technological enhancements, such as more powerful engines and instrumentation. It is equipped with an improved rotor system incorporating wide-chord blades. It is capable of executing emergency evacuation missions under difficult weather conditions, during day and night.

The built-in medical interior is installed with an integrated electronically controlled litter system to carry about six patients. This litter system can be modified to provide ambulatory seating. The helicopter also houses an integrated oxygen-generating system for onboard patient care.

F-5E Tiger II

Builder: John Chestnut

ABOUT THE BUILD

Builder:	John Chestnut
Manufacturer:	Hobby Boss
Kit Type:	F5E Tiger II
Model Scale:	1:472
Builders Home:	United States

Fast Fact:

The F-5 development effort was formally started in the mid-1950s by Northrop Corporation for a low-cost, low-maintenance fighter. The company designation for the first design as the N-156, intended partly to meet a U.S. Navy requirement for a jet fighter to operate from its escort carriers, which were too small to operate the Navy's existing jet fighters.

Iron Maiden Spitfire

Builder: Jezz Coleman

I think it's fair to say that any modelers stash is never complete unless it contains a spitfire or two. So when the opportunity arose to build this kit from Revell I jumped at the chance! this new release from Revell although it's a re-box of their original Mk II kit, the very nice addition to this set is two very well molded figures of the Iron Maiden character Eddie. One of the figures is designed to be fitted inside the cockpit as a pilot, the other one is a freestanding also supplied are two decal options one of which depicts the album cover and box art version, secondly the live stage show version which is the one I was going to be building. Before I commence with this build I decided I wanted to do something a little bit different with this and have some fun. So after some deliberation I decided that I would build this as if it was in flight, adding a small motor to make the propeller rotate. I wanted to also have the model rotating so I decided to use a turntable more about this later in the build

Not having an exact plan of how I was going to bring all of my ideas together I thought I would dive straight in, and work it out as I slowly progressed through the build.

I started off by building the cockpit area as per the instructions as this model was going to be displayed in flight i drilled a hole though the cockpit floor and glued a aluminum tube in place using two part epoxy for added strength to allow the wiring from the motor to run directly down to the battery supply that was going to be housed inside the turntable.

ABOUT THE BUILD

Builder:	Jezz Coleman
Manufacturer:	Revell
Kit Type:	Spitfire Iron Maiden Edn
Model Scale:	1/32
Builders Home:	Great Britain

Iron Maiden Spitfire

Builder: Jezz Coleman

The cockpit was painted up using Tamiya cockpit green, all the details were picked out and painted using a fine brush, a gloss coat was given to the area and following that a oil panel was wash applies to make the details more pronounced. Next up was to secure the small motor to the front portion of the fuselage, for this I used milliput that was molded into both front halves of the engine area and the small motor was pushed gently into position incased in the millliputt. With the motor in place and the cockpit also positioned

and making sure the wiring for the motor was fed down the mounting tube that was installed in the cockpit floor previously.

Revell Box Art

Iron Maiden Spitfire

Builder: Jezz Coleman

So with the technical part out the way i could carry on with the build as per the instructions, next up was the upper and lower wing sections that needs s to be fixed in to place another hole was made in the lower wing part to allow it to slide over the mounting point. The rear elevators and various parts were added as per instructions. As this build was going to built wheels up I had to modify the undercarriage slightly to allow them to be retracted. As the kit does not sadly give you the builder a much needed wheels up option.

With the main build complete and all the seams cleaned up it was time to give the model a coat of black primer, as always my preferred brand of paint is Hataka orange line range these are lacquer based, firstly I painted the underside using sky followed with some post shading of a lighter shaded of the base color to add some modulation. Once that had dried fully I masked up the lower area with Tamiya tape and applied the first of the camouflage colors I used Hataka Tan and again post shaded using various lighter shades of the base color, I then masked that using small blue-tac worms to give a soft edge between the two colors for that I used Hataka Medium Green again adding some post shading as mentioned above. With the majority of the paintwork done it was time to apply a clear coat of allclad Aqua gloss as a base for adding the decals. These went on with no issues at all with just a small amount of microsol they conformed very well to the rivet details. Another coat of aqua gloss was applied followed by a panel line wash to bring out the recessed details the excess wash was removed once dry with a soft cloth

Iron Maiden Spitfire
Builder: Jezz Coleman

It was now time to do one of star attractions of this Kit, building and painting the two superbly molded Eddie figures. Bearing in mind figure painting is not my forte I thought I did a reasonable job, I painted both figures as per the instructions color call out then gave a oil wash to further bring out the details on the figures, the pilot was glued into the seat and the painted canopy parts were also glued into position the prop was also attached to the motor with epoxy resin for added strength.

Finally I added some stretched sprue for the antenna (I know old school Modeling right there!), A final matt varnish was applied to seal the paintwork. While that was left overnight to dry, it was time to figure out how to install the model to the turntable.

After a quick brainstorm session i figured out if i turned it upside down and removing the back plate as luck would have it there was a molded support inside that perfectly fitted the aluminum tube that was supporting the model, so a hole was drilled in the baseplate above the support of the turntable the iron maiden printed base was also fixed into place on the turntable top. Finally the model was attached to the base and the wiring for the motor was attached to a battery power pack situated inside with a switch to allow the motor to be turned on and off as required. All that was left to do was give the entire model a coat of matt varnish, the masking tape was removed from the canopy and hey presto! The build was complete.

A6M1 Zero Protoftype

Builder: Snorre Sandviken

ABOUT THE BUILD

Builder:	Snorre Sandviken
Manufacturer:	Finemolds
Kit Type:	Zero Prototype
Model Scale:	1:72
Builders Home:	Norway

Boeing B-17G

Builder: Alex Green

The Builder Says:

The kit is the old Revell 1/48th B17G. I was contacted by a volunteer at the Planes of Fame museum in Chino, California and asked to build this B17, 'Kismet', for another volunteer who was a US veteran. Wilbur Richardson served as a ball turret gunner in this B17 and was wounded, putting him out action for the next mission in which the aircraft was lost over Germany.

In addition to the Kit, I used an Eduard BIG ED set for the interior, and the cockpit and forward nose interior from Resin2detail. I carefully picked which gave he most accurate representation of the subject. Along with the aftermarket sets some sections were scratch built, like the gunner steps and walkways and under the pilots seats. The Cheyenne rear turret had to be scratch built and sculpted from milliput as the later turret type was not available in the kit. The decals came from a lettering set from Kitsworld with the nose detail being hand painted. The finished aircraft was then presented to Wilbur early spring last year.

Wilbur Richardson being presented the model

ABOUT THE BUILD

Builder:	Alex Green
Manufacturer:	Revell
Kit Type:	B-17G
Model Scale:	1:48
Builders Home:	United Kingdom

Models For Heroes

SOCIAL MEDIA MODELERS REFERENCE MANUAL

Builder:

MODELS FOR HEROES

From the Author:

There is something very special about the model building community when you go online and interact with them. What is considered by some a child's hobby, is really a vibrant and flourishing hobby among adults. However, also it is now being used by some as a valuable tool to help those who have served their Countries, and also given more than anyone ever should be asked to give.

As a United States Military Veteran, I support any and all Veteran based charities and other organizations who work to help my fellow Veterans. Models for Heroes is one of them, and although they are located in the United Kingdom. Their work resonates I think all over the world. The following article and section of this book is for them, and a portion of all sales of this book will be donated to them. Hopefully the small token that I donate to them, will in some way help some man or woman who has served their Country.

These organizations do real good for those who are having trouble coping with the things they have had to sadly experience, all the while selflessly serving the Country they live in.

The act of fellow men and women who understand what is it like, to sit down with them, talk, listen and be there for them. All the while working the simple model... Seems silly to some I know. However this has such an impact. Models for Heroes is properly named. These men and women are true heroes who have given so much. I hope that the small act this book is doing helps.

The following article is by a Veteran, a man who served his Country, and who was impacted by the service. His words I hope will show exactly how valuable organizations like Models for Heroes truly are.

PAGE 062   SOCIAL MEDIA MODELERS REFERENCE MANUAL

One Heroes Story

I served in the British Army for 34 years and flew as a Helicopter pilot for 26 of those years. I began feeling out of sorts in early 2014 and was subsequently discharged medically in early 2016 with PTSD. I have spent time in a Mental Health hospital as well as poured every sinew of my heart out to various therapists both during and after my discharge. I have to be honest and point out none of my treatment has been very successful, but I understand how complex my case must be owing to the amount of built up trauma after years of service.

One of the most overwhelming changes to the human mind that is brought about by PTSD is the constant state of alert and it's such a drain on the mental energy as well as very tiring physically. The resultant affect is that I switch off to everything around me once I am safe at home. I have lost hours and days to nothing, absolutely pointless nothingness.

One day and purely by chance I decided to record my day in words and found myself writing in poetic prose which not only took me by surprise but gave me a sense of accomplishment. I didn't feel any sense of happiness about it but more a sense of purpose, that I perhaps had an ability, that maybe I hadn't had prior to becoming ill.

I began writing daily and still do today. My poems have had international as well as national success, which has been very satisfying, as I had only really written them to feed my need for being part of the world once more. Those moments of writing took me away from reality and allowed my senses to calm for an hour or two, thus allowing much needed rest but without any zombie affect.

That aside there was still something missing, something felt awkward about channeling all my spare energy into writing. I felt I needed to do something that involved my hands, something tangible and touchable. That's when I saw some online information about scale modeling, which was being promoted by "Models for Heroes" and I applied for help immediately.

So, I attended a session run by the Models for Heroes founder, Malcolm Childs and I immediately felt as ease. My mind was so consumed with the model, the glue and the paint, that it had little time to worry of daily life or threats. The very fact that the session was being run in a safe room and in a stable area meant a great deal to me. To be free of one's demons means one can run around, albeit notionally but those few hours were incredibly important toward my recovery.

I now make models at home as well as write and I think they complement themselves very well. Yes, I still have to wade through my daily routine just like everyone else but now I can take a moment here and there to recharge my mind. It has helped me so much that I now help the charity as a volunteer in order to hopefully pass on its merits.

Builder: Karl Tearney

I ought to point out I hadn't made many models as a child as financial constraints prevented that and so it all began literally from the start for me. I quickly grew from 1/72 to 1/48, from brush to airbrush, and finally onto weathering. But what really caught my attention was the cartoon type models and I have become somewhat of an addict to them all. I have completed the whole range from Meng as well as the Tiger plane models but also a few egg planes. What I enjoy most is the ease of the build and the ability to be imaginative in making the model realistic or even something artistic.

None of the toon type models require glue although I do use it at times for parts that may feel slightly loose. The plastic is very paint adhesive and often I don't even use a primer as it doesn't seem necessary.

Being introduced to modelling by Models for Heroes has helped enormously with my recovery as well as day to day management of my condition. This is especially true at night when I can be enshrouded by the madness of sleep paralysis or night terrors, as I can go to my spare room and tinker with a model which then grounds me.

Modelling has become fundamental toward my health and I am overwhelmed with the total camaraderie and support in the modelling community. Everyone I meet at shows talk so kindly and I feel truly blessed to call myself a modeler. Yes, I still have a lot to learn and to me that is one of the greatest components of modeling.

Without the generosity of the modelling community as well as manufacturers, shops and businesses I am not sure where I would be today. I am so grateful to each and every person who supports Models for Heroes as well as Malcolm who alongside his wife run the whole thing from their home and without salary.

Models For Heroes

Builder: Karl Tearney

PTSD is for me a lifelong condition and the severity of mine is not presently treatable. I remain on very powerful medicines and often reflect on when I was well. Memories can be kind but also tragic but making new memories with modelling are and will be forever good ones.

... Karl Tearney

Spitfire Mk IX

Builder: Pouillard Christophe

ABOUT THE BUILD

Builder:	Pouillard Christophe
Manufacturer:	Eduard
Kit Type:	Spitfire Mk IX
Model Scale:	1:72
Builders Home:	Belgium

Fast Fact:
D-Day Stripes

During the D-Day landings and operations allies aircraft had black and white large striped painted on their wings and also fuselages. This odd pattern was done so that allies ships, anti aircraft batteries and other allied aircraft would be able to spot fellow friendly aircaft.

In the early hours of June 6, thousands of aircraft, all bearing invasion stripes, headed for the skies over Normandy. As D-Day unfolded, friendly fire incidents were very few due to the idea of adding these stripes. And, for reasons never fully understood, the Luftwaffe failed to field any real air defenses that day, as only three German aircraft overflew the beaches that day.

Photo: Archives/Royal Air Force

With the D-Day air, land and sea operations in full swing, the invasion stripes as they were called proved a success. And by December of 1944 they were ordered removed.

FW-190A-4

Builder: Dawid Branski

ABOUT THE BUILD

Builder:	Dawid Branksi
Manufacturer:	Eduard
Kit Type:	FW-190A-4
Model Scale:	1:48
Builders Home:	United Kingdom

Fast Fact:

First entering service in late July 1942 the A-4 had the same engine as the A-3 model. However had several upgrades such as some has methanol injection systems for the engine.

It featured an MG-151 Cannon and all other armament was removed from the aircraft as part of it's "U" conversion.

There were a total of 7 A-4 variants produced, with each one adding unique upgrades, or removing others. The Germans uses the FW-190 as a real workhorse, as they produced over 20,000 of them.

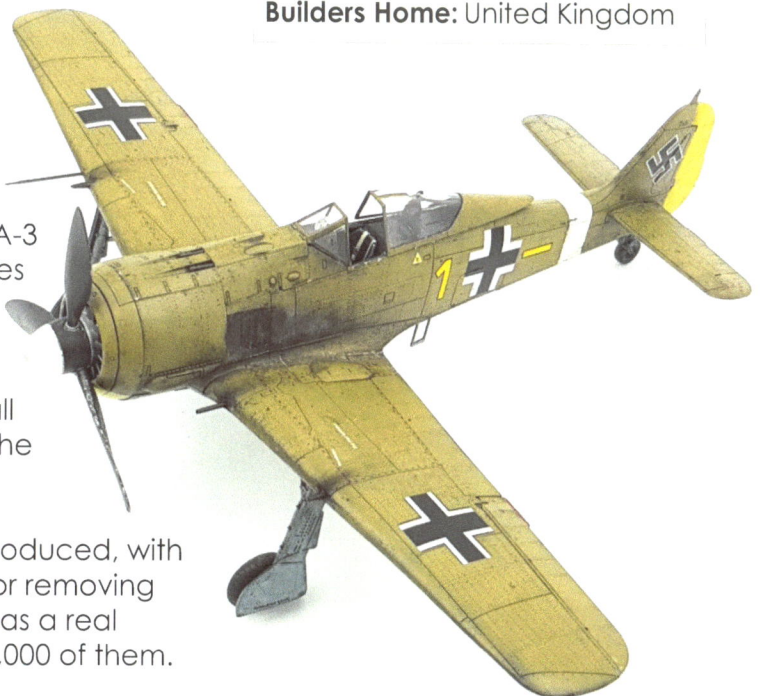

Sukhoi Su-25UTG

Builder: Rene Van Der Hart

ABOUT THE BUILD

Builder:	Rene Van Der Hart
Manufacturer:	KP
Kit Type:	Sukhoi Su-25UTG
Model Scale:	1:48
Builders Home:	Netherlands

Sukhoi Su-25UTG

Builder:Rene Van Der Hart

Fast Fact:

The Su-25UTG is a variant of the Su-25UB designed to train pilots in takeoff and landing on a land based simulated carrier deck. The first one flew in late 1988, and approximately 10 were produced.

L-29 Delfin

Builder: Snorre Sandviken

ABOUT THE BUILD

Builder:	Snorre Sandviken
Manufacturer:	AMK
Kit Type:	L-29 Delfin
Model Scale:	1:48
Builders Home:	Norway

Heavily weathered, this model shows a great example of how to make a model look far past it's prime. With chipping effects, the builder makes the model appear like it has been sitting outside for years.

Small details like the leaves on the wings add eye appeal, as does the faded canopy screen.

Snorre Sandviken is from Norway, and builds a lot of 1/48th scale aircraft. His weathering skills are top notch as you can see from this model.

Swedish Harvard
Builder: Rene Van Der Hart

Fast Fact:

Originally designated the T-6 Texan and used as a training aircraft, this plane was also used by many various Countries as a training platform and also a combat platform.

ABOUT THE BUILD

Builder:	Rene Van Der Hart
Manufacturer:	Iraleri
Kit Type:	Swedish Harvard
Model Scale:	1:48
Builders Home:	Netherlands

F-14D Super Tomcat

Builder: Alex Chambers

ABOUT THE BUILD

Builder:	Alex Chambers
Manufacturer:	Revell
Kit Type:	F-14D Super Tomcat
Model Scale:	1:72
Builders Home:	United Kingdom

Fast Fact:

The Tomcat was retired by the U.S. Navy on 22 September 2006. The F-14 remains in service with Iran's air force, having been exported to Iran in 1976. In November 2015, there were reports of Iranian F-14s flying escort for Russian Tupolev Tu-95, Tu-160, and Tu-22M bombers on air strikes in Syria

Y-Wing Bomber

Builder: John Chestnut

Fast Fact:

When designing the original model, the Y-Wing had a bubble like cockpit. However, then it was filmed with the bluescreen it did not show up. So ILM had to do a quick fix. And they came up with the cockpit that you see in the modern model.

The Y-Wing was first seen in A New Hope, the first movie made and premiering in 1977. In this movie a squadron of the ships attack the Death Star, along with Luke and the Xwings. This squadron was called Gold Squadron led by Jon Vander, they made the initial trench run attack, that was not a success. Only one Y-Wing made it out.

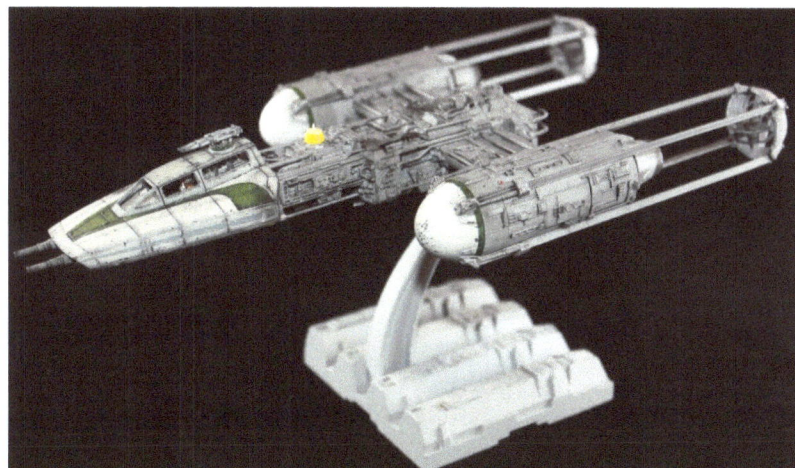

ABOUT THE BUILD

Builder:	John Chestnut
Manufacturer:	Bandai
Kit Type:	Y-Wing Bomber
Model Scale:	1:72
Builders Home:	United States

Bf109 F-4

Builder: Ben Smith

ABOUT THE BUILD

Builder:	Ben Smith
Manufacturer:	Eduard
Kit Type:	Bf109 F-4
Model Scale:	1:48
Builders Home:	Norway

Bf109 F-4
Builder: Ben Smith

The Builder Says:

I was particularly pleased with the weathered finish on this build. To achieve this I preshaded the panel and rivet lines black then mottled the panels in between with white and black. I then sprayed the RLM 78 blue in light coats allowing each coat time to dry so I could check the build up and achieve the effect I was after. The same was done with the RLM 79 desert yellow, yellow nose and white tail band.

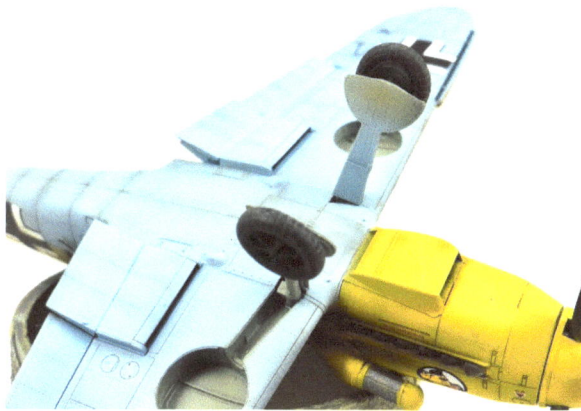

A gloss coat was applied along with the decals followed by another gloss to seal them in. Panel lines were next up, Migammo panel line wash was used here, desert sand was applied to the RLM78 and grey blue applied to the RLM 79. After these had dried I did a little post shading using Tamiya desert yellow and light blue, spraying the desert yellow in light coats over the Balkenkruez giving them a sun faded look. Next I applied a matte varnish, some desert sand powder to the underside and locked these in with another coat of varnish.

A-Wing Fighter

Builder: Donald Semora

Star Wars is an iconic movie, and as such has produced a fan base who have consistently demanded models of the ships that populate the movies. One of these ships is the A-wing.

I first got this kit a couple of years ago and I admit, I did not like it. This was not due to the kit, it was because of the paint scheme I chose. Initially I painted the model with reddish trim colors and it just turned me off to the model. However a bit ago I came across it in a box and had an idea.

I decided to take a new try at it, and I started with repainting it the base color of the creme you see.

I then did some research and decided to use a darker green as the main trim color. I was very pleased at how it turned out. I then added various decals from other kits, both modern aircraft, and science fiction based craft. This I think adds a sense of realism to it, and finally I am happy with the results. This goes to show what I feel is a valuable lesson for model builders. You should never toss in the garbage a model that you start then not like. Box it, place it away, maybe in the future you will decide that taking a new look at it is in order.

ABOUT THE BUILD

Builder:	Donald Semora
Manufacturer:	DS Custom Builds
Kit Type:	A-Wing
Model Scale:	1:24
Builders Home:	United States

BUILT BY

Ds

DONALD SEMORA

A-Wing Fighter

Builder: Donald Semora

Fast Fact:

The A-Wing Fighter colors were originally blue as was designed by Ralph McQuarrey. However, due to the blue screens used, the colors would not show up, so they switched to other colors.

Another interesting note for those Geeks out there who love Star Wars. The A-Wing was one of the only canon approved fighters, that did not show up in the attacks on the Death Star in the movies.

Cylon Hell Raider

Builder: Dina Arzapalo

ABOUT THE BUILD

Builder:	Dina Arzapalo
Manufacturer:	Moebius
Kit Type:	Cylon Raider
Model Scale:	1:32
Builders Home:	United States

Fast Fact:

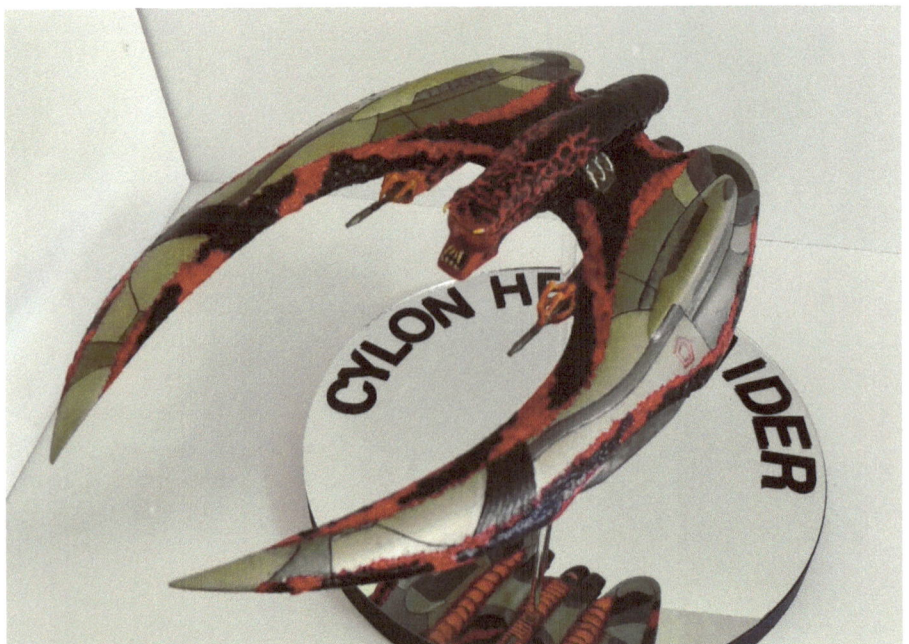

Lancaster B111

Builder: John Ashton

Fast Fact:

The Lancaster B III was powered by Packard Merlin engines, which had been built overseas in the United States, but was otherwise identical to contemporary B Is. In total, 3,030 B IIIs were constructed, almost all of them at Avro's Newton Heath factory. The Lancaster B I and B III were manufactured side by side and minor modifications were made to both marks as further batches were ordered. The B I and B III designated was effective interchangeable simply by exchanging the engines used, which was occasionally done in practice

ABOUT THE BUILD

Builder:	John Ashton
Manufacturer:	Airfix
Kit Type:	Lancaster B111
Model Scale:	1:72
Builders Home:	Great Britain

From the Author:

I scaled the model to the only size I could fit it into in my attic model room, which was 4feet 6inches long, the dam was built out of thin cereal packet card, poly-filler and model German vehicles and anti aircraft guns in the tower tops.... The display took around 4 months to build and it was built for the 70th anniversary of the raid, I also scaled up how big the model dam would be if I built the whole thing in 1/72nd scale, that would be 16feet from end to end, a bit big for my house

FLYING MACHINES
SOCIAL MEDIA MODELERS REFERENCE MANUAL

GLOSSARY OF TERMS

3D PRINTING
A relatively new form of making models. This is a process where digital files are used to literally print a part or model in specially made printers.

ABS
A type of plastic that some model kits are made or. Also, ABS is used in 3D printing as mentioned above to product homemade, or custom made models and parts.

ACRYLIC
A clear plastic use to make displays, covering for models and also canopies / glass parts.

AFTER MARKET
Products intended to supplement model kits to make them better or more detailed, this can be things like custom resin or 3D printed items, or photo etch etc.

AFV
Stands for Armored Fighting Vehicles.

BENCH
The place where a model builder makes his or her models. The Bench, can be anything from a card table in the living room, to a fully outfitted building area.

BENCH VICE
Small tool mounted to the side of a bench or work table, that is designed to hold parts that are in the process of being worked on.

BMF
A thin foil that is used to cover models to make them have a metal effect. Also called Bare Metal Foil.

BOLT COUNTER
A person who always critiques others works, focusing on minute details. Usually they themselves do not build or post images of their work. Also see Rivet Counters.

BRUSHING
When you use a brush to paint your model.

CA GLUE
Also known as Super glue, this is used many times to put 3D prints together, however also can be used on normal plastic models.

CAST
When you take a mold and pour a material in it, once cured this is called the cast.

CEMENT
Cement is a universal term for glue. There are many kind of cement out there, from CA glue, to epoxies and regular model glue.

CNC
CNC is a way of making custom parts. Using a computer design file, and a special machine that reads it. The machine uses a series of cutters to cut out of a solid block of material the part you want.

CURING
Curing is when you let something sit and become solid, or dry. This can be a casting from a mold, to allowing paint to dry.

CUTTING MAT
Cutting mats are special rubberized mats that are placed on benches. These tend to self heal, meaning once cut they seal up fairly nice.

DECAL SET
A solution that makes decals settle into small details easier.

DECAL SHEET
The sheet of paper in model kit with the decals on it. You will use water to allow them to slide off easier onto the model.

DENATURED ALCAHOL
Ethyl Alcohol (Ethanol), used to thin paint and clean up acrylic paint.

DETAILING
When you add details, and or clean up and make small details mor visible.

DIORAMA
A scaled down scene of various scenes or other real world content.

DRY BRUSH
Where a brush has almost all the paint removed until it appears dry and then is repeatedly passed over corners and high spots of a model. This shows off the raised areas and to an extent mimics the way that light reflects off corners and edges.

ENAMEL
A generic term used to describe model paints which use an oil-based thinner/reducer.

EPOXY
A strong glue, usually mixed in two parts. Once mixed well, epoxies can be a strong and effective way to make model parts stick together. They tend to be available in various curing times, anywhere from five minutes to ninety minutes.

EJECTOR PIN MARKS
On injection molded kits, metal pins are used in the mold to push out the newly formed plastic parts. The plastic is still hot and pliable so these pins create circular depressions in the plastic parts.

FDM
Stands for Fused Deposition Modeling, which is a form of rapid prototyping.

FILE
Made of metal, plastic and other materials, it is usually in some kind of stick form and has various levels of abrasive finishes. It is used to smooth plastic, resin and other materials.

FLASH
This is the overmold on plastic sprues when model kits are made. Becoming less common now, as molding techniques have improved.

HAIRY STICK
Slang for a simple paint brush.

KIT BASHING
When you take parts from several model kits to make something unique.

KNIFE
A sharp tool used to cut and trim plastic and resin.

LASER CUTTER
A specialized machine that uses a focal laser to cut materials. These machines come in various power levels, and are very dangerous.

MASKING TAPE
This tape used to trim areas when painting, where you do not want the paint to go.

MASTER
When making molds and models, the master is the main model or part of the model that you will use to make all other parts.

MINI
When making molds and models, the master is the main model or part of the model that you will use to make all other parts.

MOLD
Made of silicone or plaster, molds are used to make model parts. There are metal molds that are used in the production of large scale models commonly used in injection molding machines.

OOB (OUT OF BOX)
OOB means you are making the model with only what is in the box, and use no other aftermarket or kit bashed parts.

OOP (OUT OF PRODUCTION)
OOP is when a model kit is no longer made. They can still be available for purchase, however just are not anymore being produced.

PHOTO ETCH
Photo Etch is a highly detailed part, they come usually come on sheets of brass, and are used to add very fine details to models.

PIN VICE
Not to be confused with a "Vice" as mentioned before. A Pin Cive is a mall hand held manually powered mini-drill

PIN WASH
A pin wash is applied with a very small brush to specific areas. The wash is usually dark and allowed to flow into panel lines or around small details to emphasize them and give the impression of shadow and depth.

PLA
A plastic based material used in 3D printing that is pretty much common to use for 3D printing.

PETG
A plastic material that is used to make clear parts for models.

PUTTY
A creamy textured material used to cover and clean up seams and other imperfections in models.

REPLICA
This is a reproduction of an existing item, such as a weapon, a prop or a ship or vehicle.

RESIN
A material used to make sometimes models and model parts. Resin tends to be more brittle and hard to work with.

RIVET COUNTER
A person who always critiques others works, focusing on minute details. Usually they themselves do not build or post images of their work. Also see Bolt Counters.

SCENERY
Scenery is when you use various elements such as fake trees, or a scale building etc, to make either an outdoor scene for model displays or an indoor model display, to scale with the model you are using.

SCRATCH BUILD
When you take various parts from other models, or from things you find laying around your home or work shop, and then making a part you need for your model and or display.

SLA
Stands for Stereolithography, and is when you print in 3D using resin.

SNIPS
Small scissor like tool used to cut plastic from the sprues.

SPRUE
The tree likes structures, that model parts are attached to in model kits.

SPRUE GLUE
When you mix pieces of plastic sprue with model glue, when let sit for awhile it becomes a thick gooey material, that some model builders use to fill seams and imperfections.

STL FILE
A computer file used to print 3D parts.

WEATHERING
When you take various paints, washed and pigments and add them to a model to make it look more like it is real, and used.

WIP
Stands for Work In Progress.

WASHES
A very thin fluid used to make models look more used and old. Also is used to highlight seams, rivets and add depth to the model.

VACU FORM
Very thin plastic that is heated and then pulled via a vacuum over a wood mold called a buck. Making a part.

FLYING MACHINES
SOCIAL MEDIA MODELERS REFERENCE MANUAL

Common Model Scales

scale	1"=	Usual model types in this scale
1/4	4"	Planes, steam engine trains
1/8	8"	Die cast cars, motorcycles, trains
1/12	12"	Cars, figures, busts, motorcycles
1/16	1'-4"	Military armor, motorcycles
1/20	1'-8"	Cars, some resin figures
1/24	2'	Cars, trucks, WWI aircraft, WWII Aircraft
1/25	2'-1"	Cars, trucks, scifi resin kits (Studio scale)
1/32	2'-8"	All types of models
1/35	2'-11"	Aircraft, armor, boats, figures, diorama material
1/43	3'-7"	Metal cars and trucks - minis
1/48	4'	Aircraft, armor, O Scale Trains
1/64	5'-4"	Aircaft, S Scale
1/72	6'	Aircraft, Armor, Figures, Large Scale Scifi
1/76	6'-4"	Armor, OO scale
1/87	7'-3"	Armor, HO Scale
1/96	8'	1/8" Scale ships, aircraft
1/100	8'-4"	Aircraft
1/125	10'-5"	Aircraft
1/144	12'	Aircraft, Ships, Scifi models
1/160	13'-4"	N Scale
1/192	16'	1/16" Scale Ships
1/200	16'-8"	Boats, aircraft
1/220	18'4"	Z Scale
1/350	29'2"	Ships, scifi spaceship models
1/700	58'4"	Ships, scifi spaceship models
1/720	60'	Ships, scifi spaceship models

Size matters, it matters because the scale you choose to build in is usually determined by your budget, room for display and comfort level.

The scale of a model kit is directly promotional to the real items size. As an example. A 1/48th scale Tiger tank is about 7 inches. However a 1/48th scale German U-Boat model is almost five feet long. The below charts are designed to help you with scales.

The scales listed and the common / usual types listed are for a general reference only, and are not a complete list. There are a mixture of cars, trucks, spaceships, boats, tanks, figures and so much more in various scales.

"Studio" Scale

A note about Studio scale model building. Studio scale is not a specific size, however it references the "actual" size used for a model in a movie. These scales can sometimes be quite large. Some of these Studio Scale models cane be several feet long. A common scale however when you see the word "Studio Scale" in models is either 1/24 or 1/18.

Bandai Mech Models

Bandai has put out a widely popular series of mechs and other anime based figures. They have their own scaling system that is based on the models grade or quality. The grade and quality determines the level of detail etc of the mech or kit.

Bandai Models

Bandai MechGrade Type	General Rule on Size
1/60 Perfect Grade	Best detail Bandai makes about 12"
1/100 Master Grade	Next level of detail / quality about 8"
1/144 High Grade	About 12" - 14"
1/144 Real Grade	About 12" - 14" Quality upgrade

Bandai still manufactures the earlier kits that were first issued in the 80s. These come in a variety of sizes, from 1/220 scale to 1/60, but they are all molded in only one or two colors and need both glue (usually included) and painting to complete. Their proportions are rather different from today's kits. However there are noted exceptions, such as the Millennium Falcon they make, that they call the Perfect Version. This is in 1/72 scale and is scaled proportionally to other 1/72 scale kits. They have an entire Star Wars line in various 1/48 and smaller.

Bench Needs:

No matter the type of model you are building, there are a variety of tools that make model building so much easier. The bench is your space where you build. Some have very large and advanced spaces and some have just a small TV tray in front of their recliner. The bench is based on need, time you spend on the actual hobby, available room and really how much you want to spend. The following is a list of the tools and supplies that depending on the types of builds you do, and the space you have that you can get.

The Bench Checkist

The following are the things that model builders tend to have on their benches. Some items are not needed depending on the type of building you do. However this is a pretty comprehensive check list for reference. The list is broken into two parts, these are tools and supplies. The tools are a list of the things that will make your building life easier. The supplies are the things you need to do the models, and well... Some make your life easier also when building.

SUPPLY LIST

Glue - Plastic model type
Glue - Super glue
Glue - Glue stick type for the hot glue gun
Glue - Good old fashioned elmers
Glue - Two part epoxy - used for resin models
Blades - Have a small variety of these
Brushes - These will be based on need
Q-Tips
Small sponges
Makeup eye liner brushes - Trust me, these are great.
Small popsicle sticks for mixing etc
Small cup for mixing
Pin vice drill bits
Masking tape
Scotch tape
Rubber bands
Disposable files - Womens emery boards work great
Paint - Based on need and personal likes
Thinner medium
Airbrush thinner
Airbrush cleaner
Airbrush flow improver
Pigments various colors and tints
Panel liner - I suggest black, gray and brown
Washes - Based on personal needs
Filler putty for seams
Sticky notes for paint - See tips and tricks
Decal setting solution
Decal softener solution
Spray primer
Filler spray primer
Sand paper - Various types and grits
Mixing bottles
Eye dropper
Plastic syringe
Small pipettes
Micro mask for masking areas
Pipe cleaners

TOOL LIST

Cutting matt - Various sizes are available
Utility knife (Exacto Small Hobby Type)
Utility knife blades
Files - Metal type various sizes and shapes
Files - Disposable emery board style
Tweezers - Needle nose
Tweezers - Curved needle nose
Light of some type.
Magnifying lense
Sprue Snips / Cutters
Pin vice - Small hand drill
Pin vice bits - various sizes
Small miter box with saw
Spare miter box saw blades
Jewelers screw driver set
Pocket magnifying lese
Small clamps
Clothes pins for use as clamps
Small vice
Small hand vice
Small bins to hold things
Wire stripper
Wire gauge
Heat Gun
Hot melt glue gun
Mechanical Pencil (for scribing fine panel lines)
Small ruler
Circle template - drafting type
Small battery powered paint mixer
Air brush
Compressor
Airbrushing Vent Booth (Very important item)

THE AUTHORS BENCH

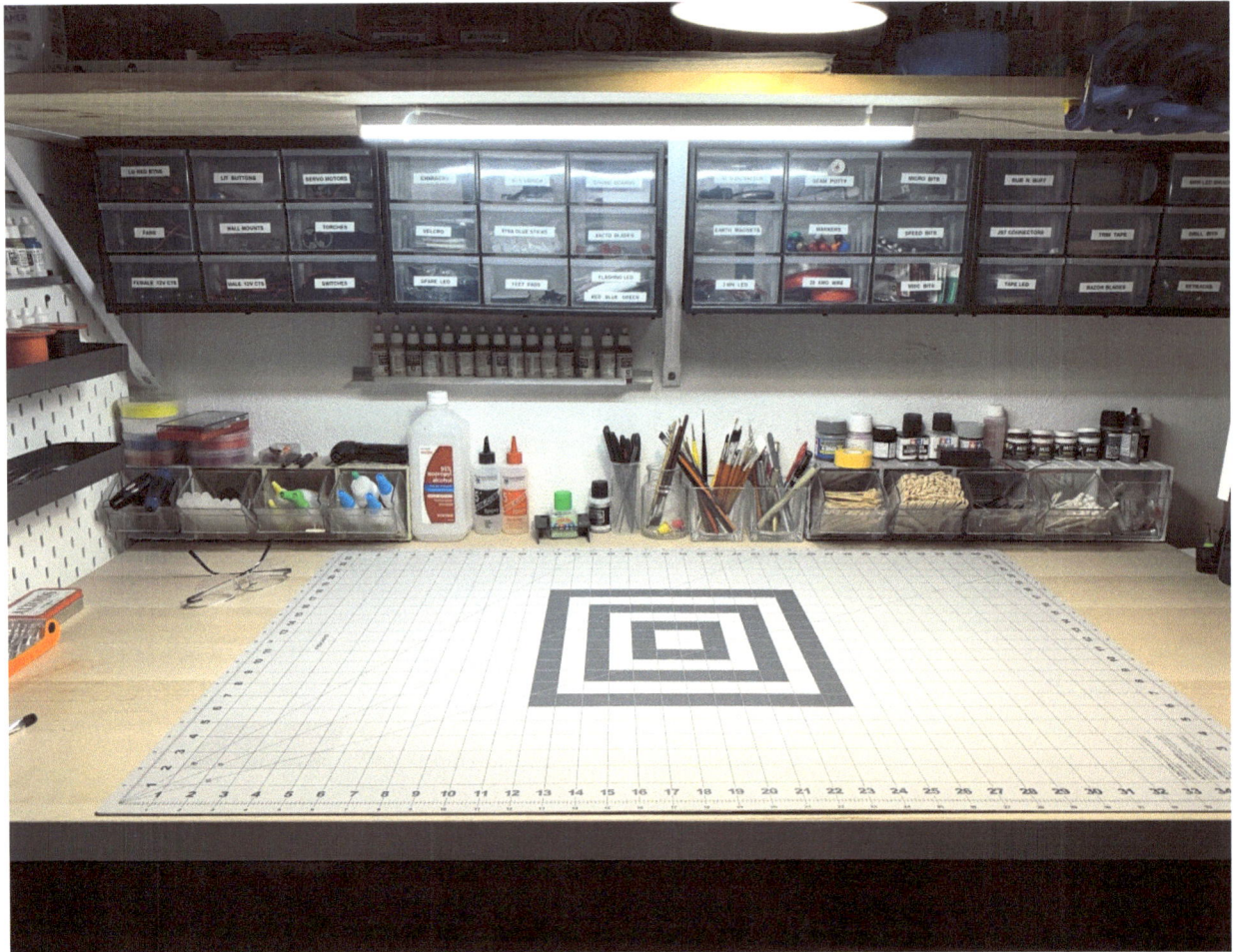

I figured I would show where my work is done on my models. Now, I have been fortunate to be able to build models for a living. I started doing it for a living about three years ago when I was approached by a collectibles company to do some work for them. I had posted some of my Star Wars builds online and the owner of the business saw it. However, as much enjoyment as that has given me, what I love more is writing.

Writing these reference manuals is a labor of love for me, as they give me a chance to meet so many other model builders and makers. They however best of all give me a chance to show so many talented builders. You the builder and the true impetus of this book. No matter if you have a bench or a simple corner of your dining room table. You are what makes this book what it is.